What Do I Want to Be?

Laurie Rozakis

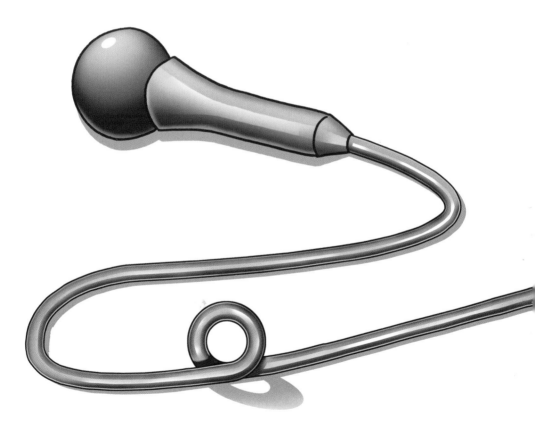

Rigby®

A Harcourt Achieve Imprint

www.Rigby.com
1-800-531-5015

Hi, I'm Zoe.

When I grow up, what will I be?

How will I know the job for me?

Who will I ask? Where will I go?

All the people in town will know.

Zoe: How are you, Mrs. Fox?

Tell me about the work you do.

Mrs. Fox: I'm a firefighter.
I must do my job quickly
to keep people safe.

Zoe: Fire fighting is exciting, I see!

But maybe it's not the job for me.

Zoe: How are you, Ms. Hall? Tell me about the work you do.

Ms. Hall: I'm a librarian. I help people find information they need for school or work.

Zoe: Librarians like to help people, I see!

But maybe it's not the job for me.

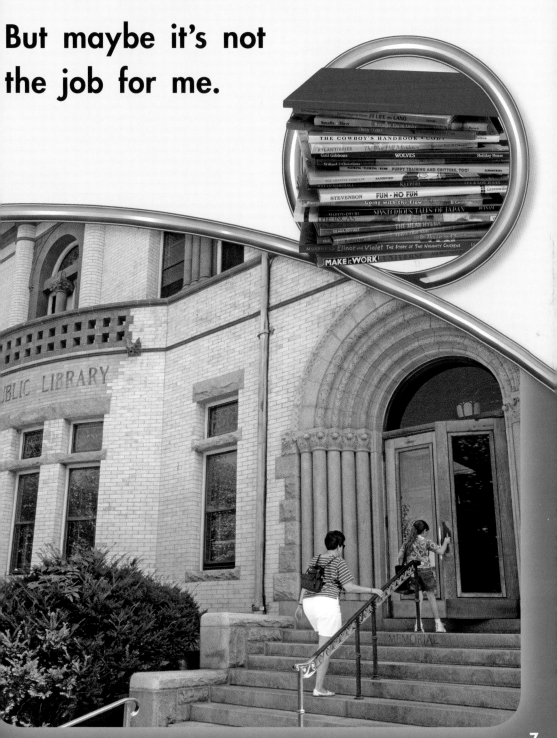

Zoe: How are you, Ms. Delp?
Tell me about the work you do.

Ms. Delp: I'm a bank teller.
The bank has many services
to keep money safe.

Zoe: Working at the bank is important, I see!

But maybe it's not the job for me.

Zoe: How are you, Dr. Cohn?

Tell me about the work you do.

Dr. Cohn: I'm a doctor.
People come to me when they are
sick and I try to make them well.

Zoe: Doctors are caring people, I see!

But maybe it's not the job for me.

Zoe: How are you, Mr. Luna?
Tell me about the work you do.

Mr. Luna: I'm a postal worker.
I deliver letters and packages.

Zoe: A postal worker works hard, I see!

But maybe it's not the job for me.

Zoe: How are you, Mr. Ford?
Tell me about the work you do.

Mr. Ford: I'm a crossing guard.
I help children cross the street
safely.

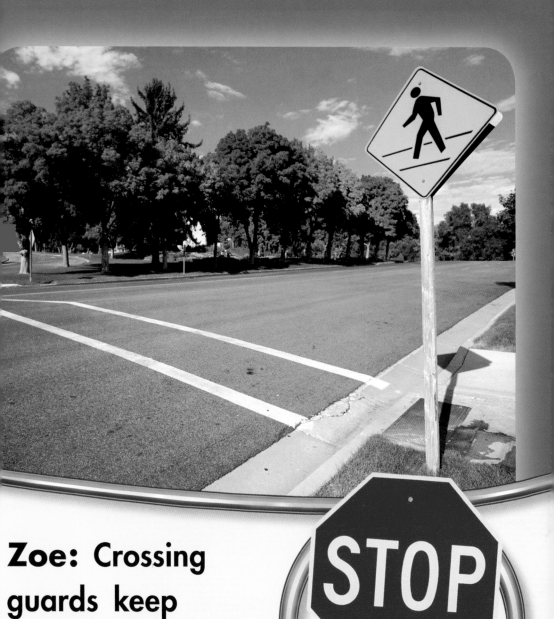

Zoe: Crossing guards keep people safe, I see!

But maybe it's not the job for me.

Zoe: How are you, Ms. Ruiz?
Tell me about the work you do.

Ms. Ruiz: I'm a teacher.
I help students learn math,
science, and reading.

Zoe: Teachers like to help kids, I see!

But maybe it's not the job for me.

Zoe: How are you, Mr. Jones?

Tell me about the work you do.

Mr. Jones: I'm a police officer.
I help keep the community safe.

Zoe: Police officers are brave, I see!

But maybe it's not the job for me.

Zoe: How are you, Dr. Rubin? Tell me about the work you do.

Dr. Rubin: I'm a veterinarian. You can bring your pet to me for shots and check-ups.

Zoe: Veterinarians like animals, I see!

But maybe it's not the job for me.

CENTURY
VETERINARY
GROUP

Interviewing is so much fun!

There's a special job for everyone.

Now I've found the job for me.

A news reporter is what I'll be!

Index